Fan Mail

Also by Joey Nicoletti

Cannoli Gangster

Reverse Graffiti

Thundersnow

Boombox Serenade

Fan Mail

from

Joey Nicoletti

Broadstone

Library of Congress Control Number 2021940411

ISBN 978-1-937968-89-2

Design by Larry W. Moore
Cover concept & artwork by the author

Broadstone Books
An Imprint of
Broadstone Media LLC
418 Ann Street
Frankfort, KY 40601-1929
BroadstoneBooks.com

For Beth, Max, Stella Bella, Roxy,

and Baruch November,

for absolutely everything.

Contents

"Baseball is reassuring. It makes me feel as if the world isn't going to blow up."

—Sharon Olds

"JUST a bit outside."

—Bob Uecker

"The one constant through all the years, Ray, has been baseball. America has rolled by like an army of steamrollers. It has been erased like a blackboard, rebuilt and erased again. But baseball has marked the time. This field, this game: it's a part of our past, Ray. It reminds of us of all that once was good and it could be again."

—James Earl Jones

"All right everyone, line up alphabetically according to your height."

—Casey Stengel

"How old would you be if you didn't know how old you are?"

—Satchel Paige

To Ted Simmons

Dear Mr. Simmons: Simba,
my grandfather never visited
St. Louis, Milwaukee, or
Atlanta, but that didn't stop him
from appreciating your gritty game
behind the plate and at bat
for the Cardinals, Brewers,
and Braves. He said
you were tougher than any bus
or Sherman Tank he drove
in civilian life and in World War Two,
and that you gunned down baserunners
as if they slept with your wife, even when
your knees felt like dinosaurs, pelted
and overcome by meteorites: their sky
ablaze, like crashed warplanes.

To Dwight Evans

Mr. Evans, I was raised to hate
all things Boston, especially
the Red Sox, by my father,
even though I had cousins
on my mother's side of my family,
the more direct European part
of my Italian American lineage,
who lived in Beantown's North End
and in Back Bay.

Had my eyebrows not been incinerated
by my father's petrol glare
when I said "Wow," after
watching you throw: when you gunned down
Sweet Lou Piniella at the dish
from Yankee Stadium's right field;
had my mother's parents not been estranged
from their Boston family members;
had I grown up there or anywhere

in New England
instead of New York,
I would have cheered for you
louder, and more often.
I would have been a Red Sox fan.
I would have worn 24,
your number, in my little league years
if my uniforms ever had them,
imagining myself at Fenway,

sharing the outfield with Fred Lynn and Jim Rice;
sharing franks and beers with friends and family
who I never had a problem with;
who were okay with teaching me
how to say Yankees suck

or I love you in authentic Italian
then chanting your nickname: Dewey, Dewey,
a dashing moustache of jet-black hope
growing on my fanatic face.

To Dave Kingman

Dear Mr. Kingman:
was it fun handing out chrome
fountain pens

to New York-based sports reporters
on your first day
of Spring Training?

This is on my mind
when I see
a small envelope

from a stranger
in Texas. I open it:
your baseball card

from 1975 has arrived,
like summer. It's in
better shape than I thought:

sharp corners, no creases
or scuffs. Then I notice
an expression of resignation

on your face,
as if posing for the picture
was necessary for you

to get on with your workday,
and my spirits sink
on your behalf,

like car keys hurled
into an ocean. Why
do I feel so connected

to someone I've never met?
How is it that being a fan
of yours: of admiring

all of the moonshots
you launched in your career,
77 of them

at the time this card was made
and distributed,
can have such an affect

on me? I mean,
would you feel empathy
for me if I got a rejection letter

from The New Yorker?
Maybe it's because I was raised
with tough love:

to hide my feelings
so that no one would use them
to hurt me, like the press did to you

when you didn't have a good game.
Maybe it's because I saw the pain
in your eyes when you struck out

when I watched you on TV
when I was a child
in my parent's house

when this card first came out,
when your image
was as constant of a presence

in my family's living room
at least as much as any adult's.
Seeing you demonstrate your talents

to perform superhuman feats:
making legendary home runs
with your bat

might have caused some to forget
that no one can be at their best
every single moment

of their work or personal lives.
As a friend of mine told me,
even computers

need down time.
As you told a reporter,
"Everyone is hot and cold, I guess."

Perhaps it's also to do with sharing—
watching ballgames with my father
and the rest of the men of my family,

with their swagger, Italian American style:
their unbuttoned polyester shirts
exposing their hairy chests,

chains, charms, and crosses,
sinking whiskey, spritzers, and beer,
having smokes, telling dirty jokes,

and swapping ballplayer stories
gave me a sense of belonging,
of being able to listen,

and converse with adults
in a common language:
horsehide vernacular.

Recalling days of yours
and my father's prime,
when you were both at your strongest,

most vibrant, and visible,
comforts me
in these uncertain days

which has exposed
how vulnerable
all of us are

and always have been.
Although I don't know exactly
how it felt

to be a young adult in 1975,
I feel for you and my father—
his focus on raising me

to be a person of steely resolve,
your focus on trying
to do your job,

to play well consistently
on the field, yet protect
your privacy off of it,

your sensitivity as powerful
as your swing,
as you try to get a hold of one

in the San Francisco cold,
The Golden Gate Bridge
gripped in mist.

To John Montefusco

Mr. Montefusco, the combination
of your Italian lineage,
your cool nickname: The Count,
your mischievous smile,
and your hatred of the Dodgers
endeared you to the men
of my family, even though you were
a San Francisco Giant
for most of your career.
I dig you for your honesty,
your willingness to tell people off;

that you didn't just burn
bridges; you destroyed them.
I dig you because you stood up
for yourself, whenever
you felt wronged, and you fought
as hard to get ready to pitch
as you did with most
of your managers—as heated
as my father (and any man
in my family could get),
his muscles twitching
backlit by the kitchen window,
sharp blinds slicing
the sun like soppressata.

To Pete Rose

Dear Mr. Rose:
even though you told me
to get lost
when I asked you
for your autograph, politely,
at Shea Stadium
when I was a teenager,
I still hope
you are enshrined
in Cooperstown someday,
because having more hits
than Ty Cobb
or anyone else
is almost
as spectacular
of an achievement
as my mother
teaching herself
and her parents
how to speak, read
and write English
as a first generation
Italian American,
in a chippy game
of cultural assimilation
where there was
no seventh inning stretch.

To Ron Cey

Mr. Cey, you captured my imagination
when I learned your nickname:

Penguin, like Batman's enemy.
You were also a reviled supervillain:

your perfect blond hair and moustache
made my mother believe and say

that Robert Redford looked like you.
This made veins bulge from my father's

sweaty neck like dead redwood roots,
almost as much as the frozen ropes

and round-trippers you smacked
against the Yankees every October—

the red face of the leather-lunged sun,
shouting across the dirty dusk horizon.

To Dick Allen
(1942—2020)

Dick, knowing that you wore
a batting helmet
when you played first base
was your way of protesting
and protecting yourself
from every so-called fan who threw
bottles and anything else
he or she could get their hands on
at you was dignity
of the highest order.

When you called out your managers
for not giving enough playing time
to some of your teammates
because they were black,
that was woke
long before woke was in vogue
to say and stay;
long before George Floyd was suffocated to death
by a cop in Minneapolis, Minnesota;
long before Michael Brown was shot and killed
by a cop in Ferguson, Missouri;
long before Eryka Badu released
her song Master Teacher:
I too, am in the search of something new
(a beautiful world I'm trying to find).

And though I could never
go yard like you
or have any idea
what it's like
or how it feels
to be black in America—
not even
in my dreams—

I can learn from you
and others
and keep learning.
I can look to you
for inspiration,
which I practice
every time I meet
someone new:

I tell that person
to call me Joey
instead of Joe or Joseph
just as you told people
to call you Dick
instead of Rich or Richie,
and I try
to speak my mind and
to make my mind as adroit,
as fast
as your hands were
when you hit the ball,
the toothless man in the moon
bracing for impact.

To Freddie Patek

Dear Mr. Patek, Flea,
you ignored insult after insult
about your diminutive size.
You ran with purpose and passion
from base to base.
You threw with power and precision
on grass and turf.
You sprayed and slapped pitches
between infielders,
and you took one deep
from time to time,
including three round-trippers
in Fenway Park
one glorious night,
the moon growing like a tumor
in the sky's ribcage.

To Mario Mendoza

Dear Mr. Mendoza, it was a treat
watching you pick it at shortstop
for the Pirates, Mariners,
and Rangers. Some people

gave you hell about
your batting average,
especially in 1979.
But The Mendoza Line:

a .200 clip is beyond the reach
of many people, including me,
who would have given anything

to have an at-bat in The Show,
much less a hit,
or 287 of them, as you had

in your MLB career, good enough
for a lifetime .215 clip. Nevertheless,
you endured more than
your fair share of teasing and

insults, like my father did
when he ran for Shop Steward
of his bus depot, having been

less academically accomplished
than his opponent. And yet,
you won fans over,

and my father won his election
and multiple awards for safe driving,
which are commemorated

in The Casey Stengel Depot, just as your
professional accomplishments are celebrated
in Salon de la Fama:

The Mexican League Hall of Fame:
a .291 lifetime clip;
the nickname Manos de Sada:

Silk Hands. The round smile
on your 1982 Topps baseball
card is a dying quail
in the left field grass
of Palacio Sultán.

To Phil Rizzuto
(1917—2007)

Mr. Rizzuto, my dear Scooter,
your quirkiness:
your digressions and musings
about cannoli, traffic
on the George Washington Bridge,
and your fear of lightning
when you called ballgames
taught me to pay attention
and listen carefully,
which came in handy
when my Nonno Giovanni spoke
to me, always
in spirited Italian,
as if I understood
everything he said,
even though I only knew
the names of foods,
cannoli being one of them,
your quick Queens wit
and Giovanni's dialect
of powdered sugar
dissolving in my ears.

To Dan Meyer

Dear Mr. Meyer: Disco
Danny, when I watched
a video of you
loosening your neck
and shaking your head, before
you hit, I remembered
my Nonna Ida,
who has been dead
for almost twenty years,
how her gnarled hands shook
when she gave me
your 1980 baseball card,
my first one of that year;
saying, *This is
for you collection.*
Then she opened
her kitchen window:
the Triborough Bridge was
awash in the melted mango
gelato of April sunlight.

To Rick Bosetti

Dear Mr. Bosetti,
has anyone enjoyed being
a Toronto Blue Jay

more than you?
This can't be measured
by any statistic

or with any known technology.
But when I see a picture
of you online, I'm taken

with the mischievous look
in your eyes; your toothy smile,
and your bushy moustache,

all of which reminds me
of my father, on a hot afternoon
at his place of work,

when he filled the air conditioner
in his boss Mr. C's office
with talcum powder,

earlier in the day.
We watched Mr. C walk
into his office. My father told me

to wait outside with him.
A minute or so passed.
Mr. C yelled

my father's name.
Then he emerged
from his office,

covered in powder.
My father asked him
if something was wrong

with the air conditioner.
Mr. C growled like a tiger
and chased him down

a stairwell, leaving a trail
of powder in the air.
That you had a vowel

at the end of your surname;
that you once had more assists
than any other centerfielder

in the American League;
that you sipped beer
as you talked to reporters;

that you claimed to have urinated
in every stadium outfield
you played in—during games—

made you seem familiar,
like a crazy uncle or cousin:
as if you and my father

would entertain each other
with your workplace banter,
as well as everyone else

gathered for Sunday dinner
or a summer cook-out;
spits of laughter

flooding the grill,
two fireflies
flickering in crab grass.

To Paul Blair

(1944—2013)

Dear Mr. Blair,
when you asked me
if I wanted you to sign
my baseball, bat,
and your rookie card,
my spirits were as high
as a moonshot smacked
by Reggie Jackson: Mr. October.
We conversed as you signed
everything. You said
it was almost as great
to be Mr. October's teammate
as it was to talk with fans
"like me," who treated you
"like family." I don't know
how or why I didn't faint,
but this memory is why
I want my body to be viewed
with the baseball you signed
in my cold, stiff hands, before
I become smoldering ash.

To Carlos May

Dear Mr. May, thank you
for helping me feel better.
Your card from 1974

took my mind off of trembling
beneath blankets and sheets
on a sweltering mid-June day,

and the metallic taste
of the thermometer that was constantly
under my ten-year old tongue

as my mother tried to make
my fever break
like the shot glass she threw

at my father
the previous night.
I wondered why

your team,
the Chicago White Sox,
had red caps like the Red Sox

used to. I also wondered
if my brother,
who was almost

a month away
from being born,
would like baseball,

and if he did,
if we would ever
oppose each other,

like you and Lee,
your brother did,
in the 1969 All-Star Game,

the first time
a pair of siblings did so
in MLB history,

at RFK Stadium,
when the Washington Senators
were still a team,

decades before
President Trump ordered
the National Guard to use

tear gas, horses, batons,
rifles, and riot shields
on peaceful protestors

to clear a path
to Lafayette Square
just so he could have a photo op

in front of St. John's
Episcopal Church;
decades before

chants of "Build that wall"
replaced "Let's go Yankees"
or "Let's go Mets" for some

of my childhood friends
and the majority
of my nuclear family;

when TV's were made
of wood, and stood
on scarlet shag carpets;

when my parents
went to bed
at the same time

or kissed each other
in public, long before
we existed.

To Rico Petrocelli

Dear Mr. Petrocelli,
I won your 1975 baseball card
in a 10-card flip.
I didn't know about you
before then, but when I read
your full name, Americo
Peter Petrocelli, on the back
of the card, I could taste
my Nonna's pizzelles, sweet
and flaky in my mouth.
When I read that you are
a Brooklyn native, I was
a Ferrari, speeding across
the Williamsburg Bridge.
I brought your card with me
as a good luck charm
when I went to Friday Night Bingo
with my grandparents. We all
won money. People mumbled.
When my grandparents died,
your card was smooth armor
in my sports coat pocket.
As I look at your picture
on this muggy, late July morning,
your smile is a turnpike,
taking me and my grandparents
to Fred's: their favorite diner.
I see this card beside a plate
packed with pancakes, four
smoked sausages, and corned beef hash,
dots of hot sauce on my sleeves.

To Rocky Colavito

Mr. Colavito, finding your baseball card
from 1958 was as joyous
as eating a plump cannoli

or my mother's baked ziti,
even though I never had the chance
to see you play. When I read

that you are a New York City native,
an Italian guy from the Bronx
who had an arm like a bazooka;

who hit the ball with thunder,
I had a new ballplayer crush.
I also wondered why none

of the men in my family
ever mentioned you.
This was back in the days

when I developed a stammer;
when my heart and brain were faster
than my tongue, which frustrated me

and some of my family members.
The view of you was from the waist up.
I marveled your broad shoulders;

your bare hands gripping a bat;
your business-like stare off to the side,
waiting for an unseen pitcher

to throw you heat,
an expression of resolve
to match your powerful build,

determined, impervious to failure,
prepared to go yard on the future.
When I showed my father your card,

my newly discovered treasure,
he raised an eyebrow.
"Rocky Colavito? I'll take

Rocky Balboa," he said.
My father's words surprised me.
He always gave props

to ballplayers of Italian descent.
Why so dismissive? This inspired me
to learn all that I possibly could
about you. The public library was

my internet, my favorite search engine,
before either of them existed.
I learned that you idolized Joe D:
Joltin' Joe DiMaggio as a child,

like my father; like many,
Italian and non-Italian boys alike.
The crack of your brawny bat

shattered in glass
of apartment windows.
Crocuses savored May sunlight

like homemade limoncello in cracked
sidewalks of pride. You signed
autographs for anyone who wanted one

after games, often for hours
on end. The Cleveland skyline swooned
every time you took one deep

or threw someone out
from right field.
The Cleveland skyline wailed

when you were traded
to the Tigers. This was
the little league team I played for

when I discovered you.
You also suited up
for the A's, the Dodgers,

and the Yankees:
your last big league team.
I wasn't sure if my father didn't know

you played for them,
or if he didn't care
to know. As I consider it now,

by the time you returned to the city,
my father was married with a child,
having started a family sooner

then he'd hoped or planned;
he was worried:
about finding a better job;

about his brother in Vietnam.
And now, as a fan of every
baseball team and stadium

in The Show, in some way,
the prospect of opening day
makes my heart swell like penne

in boiling water
more and more each year.
And while Rona has made it unclear

when the next MLB season
will begin, I have your card:
a splendid ticket stub

to hand to the usher
of my imagination. I live
in Western New York:

crowds of leaves and chickadees
always show up
and take their seats

in trees, eaves, gutters, porches,
and stay a while. I take more
deep breaths and speak slower. I look
in my oven window. My mouth waters

at the sight of my spouse's ziti, covered
with mozzarella and Parmesan cheese, browning
as it bakes on a cold, clear fall or winter night.

To Juan Soto

Dear Mr. Soto: La Fiera,
Childish Bambino,
Juan, by any name,
watching you hit:
watching you crouch,
shuffle your feet,
and smile at the pitcher
like a magician
who's about to perform
his greatest trick
is as joyous for me
as eating my spouse's baked ziti.
When you get a hold of one,
baseballs become faces
that look as if they were painted
by Salvador Dali,
and the vermilion voices of fans
kneel in your heart's cathedral.

To Razor Shines

Dear Mr. Shines: Razor,
do I have to live
a life others want
for me, just because
they've chosen it
for themselves?

When I look at your baseball card,
I see the back yard
of the house I grew up in,
where hubcaps bloomed
beside Black-eyed Susans.
I see myself

sitting at a round, burgundy
spray-painted wooden table,
slurping a glass of iced tea
as I read and memorize
the names of ballplayers
and the various cities and towns
they hail from. For instance,

Razor is your middle name.
Durham, North Carolina,
intrigued me: it was
somewhere and something different
from what I knew;
hundreds of miles away

from the constant yelling,
screaming, kicking, and punching;
from the rubber boots, pumps,
and knives the adults
in my family hurled
at each other
as well as me. Your name;

your career in The Show;
your time as a Montreal Expo
became a hope
that I could make
a different reality
for myself;

that I could find
my own way
to be present
in the moment
without knowing
precisely how

things would work out.
And I am grateful
to have this card,
this marvelous window,
where I can still see and hear
some chickadees, perched
on a clothesline; their gold chatter
cracking a concrete patio.

To Dave Righetti

Mr. Righetti: Rags, when you threw
a no-no against the Red Sox

on the Fourth of July,
my gasp zapped in a bug lamp,

hanging from the chipped red
wooden fence in my back yard,

and the booming voices of M-80's
resounded down my potholed street.

To Darryl Strawberry

Dear Mr. Strawberry,
you made the Mets
irresistible in my tweens

and teenage years
with your lethal left-handed
uppercut swing,

your cool name, and great wheels.
My mother was also a fan,
so much so, she gave me

your Sports Illustrated poster
as a reward
for making the honor roll,

before my father left her
for the final time.
Lightning bolts stretched

their luminous legs
in the excited sky
when you stepped to the dish,

and people rose
fervently to their feet
in anticipation of

a majestic moonshot
that would make
Babe Ruth

or Buzz Aldrin
clap their hands
and Herb Ritts

snap a picture
or three. One day
I watched a Mets game

with my father
in his new basement
apartment. We almost

choked on our slices
of Sicilian pizza
when we saw you

crush a ball
so hard and high
it hit the ceiling

of Olympic Stadium.
Then my father told me
to get him another beer,

another Busch from the fridge,
so he could eat, smoke, and drink
"his eyes out," and not think

about his aching back,
his next overtime shift,
the second mortgage

on the house he wasn't living in,
his blinds slicing the sun
like a radioactive pie

that no amount
of sugar or spice
could ever save.

To Graig Nettles

Dear Mr. Nettles,
when I saw you make plays
on frozen ropes
hit by Davey Lopes,
I was thrilled as an astronomer
who discovered a new planet.
When I found your rookie card
in my Christmas stocking,
my parents held hands
for the first time in weeks.
When I met you, I was happier
than a lion tamer on vacation,
and my face still hurts
from smiling the lights
out of the Buffalo skyline.

To Sal Maglie
(1917—1992)

Buon pomeriggio,
Mr. Maglie.
When I moved
to Western New York
and discovered
that your
eponymously
named stadium
is a short drive
from mine
and my family's home,
I felt comfortable,
like you did
in your Grand Island house,
unlike the batters
you delivered
lethal chin music to
when you were in
The Show,
when men wore suits
when they went
to ballparks,
or the pleasure
my Grandfather Joe took
in telling stories
about you:
Sal The Barber,
a New York Baseball Giant,
a Brooklyn Dodger,
a Cleveland Indian,
a New York Yankee,
a St. Louis Cardinal,
and a great Italian American:
a paesano, who fought

for everything he had
in his own inimitable way,
like Grandfather Joe himself,
who went from driving
a Sherman tank
in The Battle of Normandy
to driving a bus
in every borough
of New York City.
And here I am,
his namesake,
standing in line
to get in your stadium,
so I can watch
some students I work with
play for a shot
at being drafted
by a big league team,
sandwiched between
people dressed in purple
Niagara University
caps and hoodies
on an overcast, blustery
April afternoon,
a chickadee perched
on the right arm
of a barber chair.

To Lyman Bostock

(1950—1978)

Dear Mr. Bostock: Abdul Jibber Jabber,
when your batting average was .147,
you asked Gene Autry not
to pay you. He said no.
You gave your monthly paycheck
to charity, and you did this in a time
when money was tight for many
in America, including my family,
when my father couldn't work
because he broke his back,
just as you did every time you suited up
for the Twins and Angels,
a halo of mosquitoes
buzzing above a bird bath
filled with beer cans and bullets.

To Vince DiMaggio
(1912—1986)

Dear Mr. DiMaggio,
I wish I could have heard you sing
when guests asked you to do so
at your family's restaurant. Your swing
had a hole, but you smacked
125 homers during your stay
in The Show. Fans packed
Forbes Field to watch you play.
You and the Pirates fought
over money spent on a steak,
which is why you sought
a trade; a clean break.
You went down swinging.
You never stopped singing.

To Satchel Paige
(1906—1982)

Dear Mr. Paige,
            the only regret I have
about being born
            when I was
is that I didn't get to see you pitch
                        in a live game;

to see you throw
            your Jump Ball,
                        Be Ball,
        Two-hump Blooper,
Midnight Creeper,
            Bat Dodger,
                or Hesitation   Pitch,

I would have loved to hear
            you tell Jackie Robinson
and the rest
            of your infielders
and outfielders
            to sit down
while you struck out the side.

I would have loved to see
                        you intentionally walk
two batters
            in the 1942 Negro League World Series,
so you could face
            the great Josh Gibson
with the bases   loaded
                        and tell him where
each pitch was going to go
        before
you struck him out
            on three straight pitches.

It would have been beautiful
                to watch you help
Cleveland
                win
                        the 1948 World Series,
months after
                        my mother was born—

with other pitches,
                    such as a screwball,
            knuckleball,

and the Eephus pitch;
                my jaw dropping
like a drawbridge;

people embracing
                in the Terminal Tower,

and every single fountain
                        in Kansas City
        gurgling your name.

To Jimmie Crutchfield
(1910—1993)

Dear Mr. Crutchfield:
I never saw you
catch fly balls barehanded.
I never saw you
steal bases or stretch
singles into doubles or triples.
But tonight, when I see

Comet Neowise
zoom past moons and planets,
I imagine you, running
the bases in Greenlee Field;
stars foaming
in a clear Pittsburgh sky
like a radiant round of beers.

To Tony Lazzeri
(1903—1946)

Mr. Lazzeri, my Grandfather Joe told me:
his pride in being a first-generation Italian
American was never greater,
never more swollen
than when you hit two grand slams; "two
Grand Salamis" in a game; the first
person to do so in The Show,
and you also had another round-tripper
that day in May
of 1936; and he met Mary,
his future wife,
my grandmother that night,
who made his jaw drop
like a fire escape ladder
on an Arthur Avenue walk-up.

To Lee Mazzilli

Mr. Mazzilli, in a decade when Al Pacino,
Robert DeNiro, Sylvester Stallone,
and John Travolta stirred audiences
with their respective performances

in Dog Day Afternoon,
The Godfather, Part Two,
Rocky, and Saturday Night Fever,
your thick, wavy jet-black hair,

brown eyes, olive skin,
and muscular physique
made my mother weak
in the knees—

made her say
that you and I looked alike.
I tried not to laugh.
You also gave the men

of my family
another source of ethnic pride.
You were the latest
in what seemed to be

a hit parade
of American pop culture icons
of Italian descent
whose careers were established

in the 1970s,
the decade of my childhood.
You wore eyeglasses
at the dish. This discovery

made me feel better
about being compared to you,
because I saw you
as you were:

a young Italian American man
from Brooklyn: Sheepshead Bay,
rather than the deity
my mother and others

had made you out to be.
You were adored by Mets fans.
You were the first big leaguer I saw play
in their prime, whose last name ended

in a vowel, like mine does,
and whose imperfections
were noticeable. All
of your Hollywood leading man looks

and athleticism couldn't overcome
your need for glasses
to make the most
of your baseball talents.

Both of my parents adored you.
A case in point: my mother
sent me and my father
on an errand. We picked up milk,

semolina bread, smokes,
and a three-pack of baseball cards,
where you could see some
of the players' cards. They were

in an endcap
in McCrory's, my favorite
five and dime store.
We searched through each rack

like archeologists
searching for a buried city.
My father grabbed a pack
with your card: your smiling face

in the middle one.
You looked toward the left;
camera flash glimmer in your
Adriatic eyes. The picture radiated

confidence, as well as
a boyish charm.
It seemed to express
a curious combination

of poise and pride,
in the person you had become.
For all of my mother's claims,
you and I had black hair, brown
eyes and tawny skin in common,

but that was it. Otherwise,
you looked how I wanted
to feel: self-assured; happy
in my own skin. Calm,

as opposed to worrying
when my parents would have
their next argument that escalated
into dishes being hurled,

then pushing and punching. Maybe
I'll get there, I thought to myself.
Maybe I will feel as good about myself
as Lee does when I'm older. Hold on

to this one, my father said.
It will be valuable someday.
He handed me the three-pack.
I put it on the rusted shopping cart seat,

a kiss of Neon green
light on my father's thick neck.

To Yu Darvish

Dear Darvish-San,
you throw hard.
You have a name for the ages.
You shatter the stained glass
of my cathedral imagination
when you take the hill,
and a gun metal-gray cloud
tightens its grip on the sun.

To Frank Viola

Dear Mr. Viola: Sweet Music,
Robert Frost posited
that pitchers are like poets.

If that's so, then I'll bet
you can write a sonnet or canzone
that's as mean as your fastball

and your circle change was,
both of which made hitters
swing, miss, and grab

more pine than workers
at a Christmas tree lot,
and say quick prayers

in on-deck circles,
trying not to obsess
over your Vesuvius

of a left arm, the prospect
of your controlled, sonorous
lava oozing in their heads.

To Rusty Staub
(1944—2018)

Dear Mr. Staub,
or Le Grand Orange:
If I could cook

half as well as you,
If I could hit
one-tenth as well as you,

I would be happier
than any man or woman
drunk on Hurricanes

during Mardi Gras.
You learned French
when you played

for the Montreal Expos
so you could converse
with the city's fans

and reporters.
You showed
new Mets teammates

around New York City
and helped them find
places to live

and you helped
the widows and children
of 9/11 first responders

pay their bills.
I didn't have
the chance to eat

at your restaurant,
but getting to see some
of your hits as an Expo,

Detroit Tiger, Texas Ranger
and a Metsie was
as much of a treat

as my spouse's Cozze Bianco
on Christmas Eve,
streetlights ripening

like grapes
in the vineyard of night.

To Manny Mota

Dear Mr. Mota,
when your name was announced
in Game 1 of the 1978 World Series,
the fans cheered for you loudly
at Chavez Ravine, and so did my uncle
when he saw you tip your cap
to the crowd. My father said
you were the only Dodger
he didn't hate. I asked why.
He told me to watch, wait,
and see. Then you became
MLB's all-time pinch-hit king
the following season. I began
to understand, one single
at a time. My new joy was
getting your baseball card
from 1979: an onion ring
from Burger King
around your head
like a fried frame.

To Bo Jackson

Dear Mr. Jackson: Bo,
watching you break a bat
over your helmet
aroused feelings of sympathy
in me for any pitcher
you took deep,
as well as for Brian Bosworth,
after you shoved him
to the Kingdome turf
on Monday Night Football,
my family's dishwasher humming
a requiem of soap and suds
that might never have ended.

To Al Rosen
(1924—2015)

Dear Mr. Rosen:
reading the back
of your 1954 baseball card

this breezy afternoon
on my back porch
provides relief from the pirrahnas

gnawing at my stomach. Then
I gasp. You not only won
the American League MVP award

in 1953, the vote
was unanimous.
I first became aware of you

during your days
in the Yankees front office,
in the late 1970's,

when I came of age
as a baseball fan.
My father told me:

you were a 4-time All Star selection
in your 10-year career,
all of which were spent

with the Cleveland Indians:
The Tribe, as I learned.
Not only were you among the best

players in The Tribe's history,
you were also among the greats
of your era, renowned

for your toughness
and power swing.
Back and leg injuries

hastened your retirement.
My father spoke with reverence
about you and your accomplishments,

which was unusual,
as his Yankees fanaticism
usually precluded him

from acknowledging,
much less speaking well
of ballplayers who never wore

Yankee pinstripes
or road grays.
Your part in helping form

the Bronx Zoo Yankee teams
endeared you to him
as well as me,

which is why
we were excited
as a pair of bumper cars

colliding in a carnival
under a cotton candy-pink dusk
when I first showed him

this baseball card.
My father recently celebrated
another birthday. You

are no longer here,
but my father still is,
and your card reminds me

that change is not
only inevitable,
it can also be met

with joy, optimism,
and solemnity,
a lesson that I am grateful

to have learned,
to try to practice,
and to always

bear in mind,
including today,
my stomach's pain dissipating

as I imagine a time
when playing hurt
was a point of pride;

an invisible medal
on dirt-stained uniforms;
the thought of getting older

as a privilege
that some never get to enjoy,
like playing baseball for a living,

blossoming in my mind
like gray hairs
in my scruff's garden.

To Jimmy Wynn
(1942—2020)

Mr. Wynn, I never knew
that you were the first Houston Astro
to go yard three times
in the Astrodome,

or that you were an All-Star
more times with the Los Angeles Dodgers
than any other ballclub
you suited up for, including

my beloved New York Yankees.
You had a sharp batting eye.
You had a strong arm.
You had two marriages and
you had a great nickname:

The Toy Cannon,
which made Houstonians proud,
and thrilled my good friend Steve
when you threw him a ball

and smiled when he caught it
in the bleachers of Shea Stadium:
the Big Shea, which makes us both cry
as we see your obituary in the Times

this overcast, pandemic morning,
the 2020 baseball season's postponed start
feeling like an acid rain delay
in an abandoned stadium
of our cheap seat souls.

To Anthony Rizzo

Dear Mr. Rizzo,
che diavolo?
When you gave hand sanitizer
to Orlando Arcia

after he reached first base
on opening day, which was
long awaited by many in 2020,
my spirits were lifted, as if I stood

in an elevator destined
for the top floor of Willis Tower,
because it seemed
like an act of kindness,

something to ease
people's anxieties and pains,
in a time where thousands
of people are dying

from the coronavirus each day,
including MLB fans;
in a time where people are pulled
off of city streets,

like Mark Pettibone in Portland
by secret police, who locked him up
in a holding cell, only to release him
without any explanation. Then I read

that you shared your sanitizer in jest;
that you like to "joke around"
and "keep it loose."
This was your way of being funny,

which is apparently better
than being genuinely kind
and compassionate,
even considering that all of us

are in "unusual circumstances."
Tell me this, paesan: if you
or someone else
you actually care about

gets the virus,
will you want
that person's doctor to laugh
as he or she gives the prognosis,

which could mean the end
of that person's life, considering
that there's no vaccine yet,
just to keep it loose?

To Frank Catalanotto

Dear Mr. Catalanotto:
you are the Sultan
of Smithtown Swat.
You played left field,
first, and third base
as dexterously
as Mike Massimino spacewalked.
You hit the ball
with determination,
as if you were grinding
through traffic on the L.I.E.;
the shooting stars of line drives
crashing in Arlington alleyways
and gaps, nebulas of dust
and dirt rising
as you run and slide,
Long Island Sound water
streaming through
your San Margherita veins.

To John Pacella

Dear Mr. Pacella: Johnny P,
as my father called you
when he watched you pitch on TV
in your big league debut,
your passion for the game, for playing
in New York, your home
state, was palpable. You fired
throw after throw
as hard as you could.
You weren't a Metsie for long,
but you made my father ecstatic,
knowing that an Italian guy
from Long Island:
The Guyland could make it
to The Show, like you did
when you were 21,
your hat falling off
after every throw.

To Kent Tekulve

Dear Mr. Tekulve:
Teke, how could I
or any other baseball fan

in his or her right mind
not love you?
Your unusual first name;

your prescribed, stylish shades;
your lanky physique
and your killer submarine delivery

gave you the appearance of a diabolical
high school biology teacher
on the hill, closing games

with more accuracy than heat;
my grandfather, cheering
you on, calling you Clark Kent

when you pitched the final out
of the 1979 World Series, cigar smoke
fogging the mirrored living room wall.

To Lenny Randle

Dear Mr. Randle,
as cool as it is
that you are the first

former big leaguer
to play professionally
in Italy;

as entertaining
as it was to watch you
blow the ball foul

in the Kingdome,
I will never forget
the moment I started

rooting for you.
My father's hatchback hobbled
into the driveway.

My grandfather downed pills
for his heart
and a handful

of pistachios
for his mouth
as we watched

the New York Mets:
the Metsies play the Giants:
Los Gigantes,

who were winning,
on TV. And you,
my grandfather's

new favorite Metsie,
tried to slide back
into first base. My father

joined us on the couch.
His cheer of Go
Lenny Quick, go rose

in a wave of dirt
just before the umpire
called you safe. We were

seven innings deep
into that ballgame,
but sunlight sprayed

the outfield of possibility,
and the coast to coast
smile on your face

was a bottle of cold
beer: Rhinegold
in my father's hand;

the shrapnel
of pistachio
shells in my grandfather's lap.

To Gorman Thomas

Dear Mr. Thomas,
your long auburn hair
flowed from your cap,

like beer on tap
at bars and concession stands.
And when I saw you step up

to Milwaukee County Stadium's
proud plate, the crowd's royal blue
and gold cheers bloomed

in goose pimples on my arms.
Bernie Brewer stood
on the top of his slide

in foamy anticipation
of you taking one deep,
August sunlight spreading

across the afternoon sky
like your mustard-based
barbecue sauce.

To Sal Fasano

Mr. Fasano, you wore many uniforms
in your career
in The Show:
Royals. Phillies.
Yankees, A's,
and Blue Jays,
to name a few.
You rocked your tapered tendril
moustache; you called
a good game,
and you and your spouse named
your sons Santino,
Angelo, and Vincenzo.
You took one deep
in a game I saw
in Kansas City:
the smile on your face
as you rounded the bases
was as sweet and delightful
as my mother's Tiramisu.

To Mark Fidrych
(1954—2009)

Mr. Fidrych, you were the most
fun player I ever saw,
not just because you talked
to yourself in between pitches
as you gripped the ball;
not just because you patted
the dirt on the hill
on your hands and knees,
but also because fans, writers,
and teammates
called you The Bird,
after Sesame Street's Big Bird,
who I watched as a child
with Candy: my playful poodle
until my mother came home
from work, bags
under her eyes; enjoying
a glass of wine with dinner,
me and Candy walking
after the dishes were washed,
maples drunk on rainwater.

To Bruce Kimm

Dear Mr. Kimm,
your hard-nosed play
made me root for you
even more than the fact
that you were
Mark The Bird Fidrych's
personal catcher.
Watching you block the plate
and call games
for the Chicago White Sox
as well as you also did
for the Detroit Tigers
was like watching my Uncle
Michael sing and dance
on stage: captivating,
passionate, powerful, inimitable,
and appreciative
of any chance to perform
lead or backup vocals
on covers of Motown hits,
precise and moving
as a Bird sinker
into your scuffed,
broken-in mitt.

To Tommy John

Dear Mr. John: I saw an episode
of *The Six Million Dollar Man*,
one of my favorite childhood shows,

on TV this afternoon. It was fun.
That said, the way I figure it,
if Lee Majors will live forever

in reruns for playing a secret
agent: Steve Austin, who became
"better, stronger, faster" than he was

before groundbreaking surgery,
then you should be immortalized
in Cooperstown for earning most

of your career wins after you had
surgery that bears your name. That
you accomplished this at all, much

less in 26 years astonishes
me, and not just because I enjoyed
watching you pitch in Dodger blue

and Yankee pinstripes as much as
I enjoyed watching Steve Austin,
especially when he worked with

Oscar Goldman and Jamie Sommers, just
as you did with Tommy Lasorda,
Steve Yeager, Joe Ferguson, and

Jerry Grote, but also because
your career lasted longer than
my parents' marriage. They tried. You

persisted, which is more than many
can dare think or say, even if
their tendons and ligaments are

still intact, complaining, like me
when my internet speed
is slow and I have to reboot

my modem, annoyed that the last sound
I hear is *boo-boo-boo-boo-boo*
before Steve Austin vanishes.

To Bob Watson

(1946—2020)

Mr. Watson, you will always be the first
player to hit for the cycle
in both, the National and American League;
the second African American General
Manager, and the first one
to win a World Series Championship.
But I love you for being the man
who inspired the chant, "Let them play"
at the Astrodome,
when the Bad News Bears took
on the Houston Toros
and my father promised
we would go
to a ballgame together
as soon as his broken
back was healed,
his meaty hand on my shoulder,
scoreboards of joy
exploding in my eyes.

To Gene Richards

Dear Mr. Richards,
I learned how to choke up
on the bat
by watching you on TV.
So when I tried it in
a little league game,
I got my first hit of the season,
a ground ball with eyes,
which I tried to stretch
into a double by running
as fast as I could, like you did,

which might have worked if
I had your speed
and baserunning acumen,
and if the burly left fielder didn't
gun me down
like a shabby outlaw
in a spaghetti western
before the credits fell
in the darkness
like too many stars
to wish upon.

To Lenn Sakata

Dear Mr. Sakata,
you were as versatile
as a Swiss Army knife.
You seemed to understand baseball
as well as Carl Sagan understood
the universe, which inspired me
to learn how to bunt
and get in front of every ball hit
to me at second base, shortstop,
third base, and left field, regardless
of how many errors I made
in pickup or little league games,
or all of the times my father
and my friends rolled their eyes
when I sang your praises
like an overeager opera singer
at the Met on opening night
every time we saw you play
in person or on TV, lemon
Italian ices melting on my tongue.

To Biff Pocoroba
(1953—2020)

Dear Mr. Pocoroba:
you had a fantastic name
and you called a good game,
which made me watch

the Atlanta Braves
with added interest
when I was a child.
After you retired,

you started a business
where you made sausages
like your Nonno did
for you and your famiglia

when you were a child,
like my Nonna did
for me and my *famiglia*,
which stuffs me with sorrow

as I read your obituary,
as if I lost a *zio*
who I never had
the pleasure of meeting.

To Mookie Wilson

Mr. Wilson, I have been a fan of yours
since I saw your name
on the scoreboard of Big Shea Stadium
with my Uncle Michael, back in the day
when he was still alive, before
anyone knew the full extent
of the damage that was done to him
by Agent Orange.
We loved your wheels and
your hustle, which made us jump

out of our seats when Hubie Brooks
drove you home
to win a game against the Dodgers,
which made it rain
peanut shell shrapnel
in the right field upper deck;
pearls of sweat sliding
down our Neapolitan necks;
the basepaths of my family history
dotted with spike prints.

To Willie McGee

Mr. McGee, you looked as if
you got a whiff
of a rotten cheese factory
on fire, especially when
you stepped to the dish,
but I guess it was
your game face,
your look
of intense concentration,
which made you fun to watch,
and my friend Matty-Ass
raise an eyebrow
when he learned
the Yankees traded you
to the Cardinals,
his blue groans crashing
through expressway sound walls.

To Gary Thomasson

Dear Mr. Thomasson,
when I was 8
I wanted nothing more

than to get your 1979
baseball card. I needed it
to complete that year's set,

but no one I knew had it,
including my best friend
Phil, despite all

of the wax packs we bought
from the ice cream man
that suspenseful summer.

You were my white whale;
a World Series champion;
a New York Yankee

for 9 months,
which was long enough
for me to appreciate

and admire your ability
to play everywhere
in the outfield,

your quick bat,
and your grit.
When I finally

got your card,
Phil and his family moved
to another state. I cried

for two weeks.
I had no idea
if Phil and I would ever

hang out again,
but your card gave me
something else to talk about

when we wrote letters
to each other, in a time
when phones were in walls;

when my mother dried laundry
on a clothes line, breeze-blown
aquamarine beach towels
waving goodbye and hello.

NOTES

All statistics come from www.baseball-reference.com.

The Bob Uecker quote comes from the 1989 film *Major League*, which was written and directed by David S. Ward.

The James Earl Jones quote comes from the 1989 film *Field of Dreams*, which was written and directed by Phil Alden Robinson.

"To Dwight Evans" uses the baseball term "the dish," which refers to home plate.

Quotes and information used in "To Dave Kingman" come from the New York Times article, "Kingman Appears to Erase the Past", which was written by Joseph Durso and published in The New York Times on March 9th, 1981.

"To Ron Cey" uses the terms "frozen ropes" and "round trippers." In baseball parlance, a frozen rope refers to a hard hit ball by a batter, which is also known as a line drive. A round tripper is a home run, which is also referred to as a "big fly," "bomb," "blast," "dinger," "ding dong," "four-bagger," "goner," "jack," "jonrón," "longball," a "mashed tater," "moonshot," "no-doubter," "oppo boppo," "poke," and "yicketty." The act of hitting or having hit a home run is often referred to as "knocking it out of the park," "going/went yard," "went bridge," "taking a pitcher downtown," "take one/ took one/went deep," and "went long."

"To Dick Allen" uses the Eryka Badu lyrics, "I am in the search of something new" and "(a beautiful world I'm trying to find)". These lyrics are in her song "Master Teacher," which appears on her 2008 album, *New Amerykah Part One (Fourth World War)*. This poem also uses information from the Bleacher Report article "Dick Allen: What Could Have Been", which was written by Cody Swartz and published online in Bleacher Report on April 29, 2009.

"To Mario Mendoza" uses the term "dying quail." This refers to a ball that a batter hits softly and drops in front of one or more fielders.

"To Dan Meyer" is for Ida D'Alleva.

Information used in "To Rick Bosetti" comes from the *Baseball Hot Corner* article "Where Are They Now? Rick Bosetti", which was written by Douglas Fox and published online in Baseball Hot Corner on February 18th, 2015.

"To Tony Lazzeri" uses the terms "Grand Slam" and "Grand Salami." They both refer to home a run hit when the bases are loaded; when there are runners on all three bases. This poem is for Arnold Toback.

"To Yu Darvish" uses the term "The hill." In baseball parlance, this refers to the pitcher's mound.

"To Frank Viola" references the following Robert Frost quote: "Poets are like baseball pitchers. Both have their moments. The intervals are the tough things."

"To Dave Righetti" uses the term "no-no." In baseball parlance, a no-no refers to a no-hitter, which is when one or multiple pitchers do not give up a hit in a complete baseball game of nine or more innings.

"To Sal Maglie" uses the Italian phrase, "Buon pomeriggio," which translates to "Good afternoon" in English.

"To Rusty Staub" is for Karen Mazza and James Toback.

"To Manny Mota" is for George Guida.

"To Jimmy Wynn" uses information from the SABR (Society for American Baseball Research) Biography "Jim Wynn", which was written by Mark Armour and published online in the SABR Research Collection on June 5, 2014.

"To Anthony Rizzo" uses the Italian phrase, "Che diavolo," which translates to "What the hell?" in English. The poem also uses quotes and information from the Marquee Sports Network Article "Anthony Rizzo rolls out hilarious hand sanitizer gag at first base", which was written by Tony Andracki and published online in *Marquee Sports Network* on July 24, 2020.

"To Frank Catalanotto" refers to the L.I.E., which is an abbreviation for the Long Island Expressway, and is officially known as Interstate 490 in the state of New York.

"To Lenny Randle" is for Joseph M. Nicoletti, Sr.

The quoted words in "To Tommy John" are part of the narration in the opening sequence of the television show *The Six Million Dollar Man*, which aired on the ABC television network from 1974-1978.

The quoted line in "To Bob Watson" comes from the 1977 film *The Bad News Bears in Breaking Training*, whose screenplay was written by Paul Brickman.

"To Gene Richards" uses the phrase "a ground ball with eyes," which refers to a ball that inches beyond the reach of one or more fielders and allows a batter to get on base successfully.

"To Biff Pocoroba" uses the Italian words "famiglia" and "zio," both of which translate to "family" and "uncle" in English, respectively. This poem also uses information from the Aol.com AP (Associated Press) column, "Remembering an old family friend, Biff Pocoroba," which was written by Paul Newberry and published on May 28, 2020.

"To Bruce Kimm" and "To Mookie Wilson" are for Michael Nicoletti.

"To Gary Thomasson" is for Phil LeClare.

Acknowledgments

Many thanks to the journals and blogsites in which the poems below first appeared, sometimes in different forms:

Ball Durham: To Al Rosen, To Lenn Sakata

Big Windows Review: To Paul Blair

Cacti Fur: To Razor Shines

The Daily Drunk: To Gorman Thomas

Green Hills Literary Lantern: To John Pacella, To Rusty Staub, To Mookie Wilson

Ovunque Siamo: To Rick Bosetti, To Frank Catalanotto, To Vince DiMaggio, To Sal Fasano, To Tony Lazzeri, To Dave Righetti

Paterson Literary Review: To Biff Pocoroba, To Phil Rizzuto, To Rico Petrocelli

Pembroke Review: To Jimmy Wynn

Red Eft Review: To Lyman Bostock

Stymie Magazine: To Dwight Evans, To Dave Kingman, To Satchel Paige, To Ted Simmons

Trouvaille Magazine: To John Montefusco

Turnstyle: The SABR Journal of Baseball Arts: To Ron Cey, To Jimmie Crutchfield, To Gene Richards

Wild Violet: To Pete Rose

I am immensely grateful to Larry Moore for his faith and support of my work and to the wonderful staff of Broadstone Books for bringing this book into the light of publication day. Grazie di cuore.

Endless busloads of thanks to the friends whose ceaseless sagacity, generosity, kindness and encouragement helped immeasurably in the making of these poems: Baruch November, George Guida, Maria Mazziotti Gillan, Mary Beth Sullivan, Janine Certo, and Lawrence Baldassaro.